level **2**

Combine Harvesters

D1494346

Hannah Wilson

KINGFISHER

First published 2015 by Kingfisher
an imprint of Macmillan Children's Books
20 New Wharf Road, London N1 9RR
Associated companies throughout the world
www.panmacmillan.com

Series editor: Polly Goodman
Literacy consultant: Hilary Horton

ISBN 978-0-7534-3873-2

9 8 7 6 5 4 3 2

2TR/0917/WKT/UG/105MA

A CIP catalogue record for this book is available from the British Library.

Printed in China

Picture credits
The Publisher would like to thank the following for permission to reproduce their material:
Top = t; Bottom = b; Centre = c; Left = l; Right = r
Cover Shutterstock/smereka; 4 Shutterstock/My Portfolio; 5t Shutterstock/Svitlana-ua; 5b Shutterstock/
Pefkos; 6 Shutterstock/vladimir salman; 7 Shutterstock/Leonid Ikan; 8–9 Shutterstock/Ratikova;
8t Shutterstock/Perutskyi Petro; 9t Shutterstock/Kletr; 10–11 KF Archive; 12–13 Shutterstock/mihalec;
14l Shutterstock/Pefkos; 14–15 KF Archive; 15t Shutterstock/Ruud Morijn Photographer; 16 Shutterstock/
muratart; 17t Corbis/Christophe DI PASCALE/Photononstop; 17b Shutterstock/TwilightArtPictures;
18–19 Shutterstock/abdulrazak; 19t Shutterstock/Bullwinkle; 20 Getty/Roelof Bos; 21t Getty/Kevin Day;
21b Superstock/Design Pics; 22t Shutterstock/vladimir salman; 22m Shutterstock/Leonid Ikan; 22b
Shutterstock/mihalec; 23t Shutterstock/Pefkos; 23m Shutterstock/muratart; 23bl Corbis/Christophe DI
PASCALE/Photononstop; 24 Corbis/Bettmann; 25t Wisconsin History; 25b Wisconsin History; 26 Corbis/©
Lucas Schifres/Visuals Unlimited; 27 Shutterstock/surachet khamsuk; 28–29 CLAAS KGaA mbH; 29t with the
kind permission of Francis Godé; 30–31 Flickr/Russfeld.

Contents

What is a combine harvester?

A combine harvester is a big machine. It cuts and collects plants that grow on a farm. We call these plants **crops**.

This combine harvester is cutting a crop called wheat. It cuts the wheat and collects the **grains** inside.

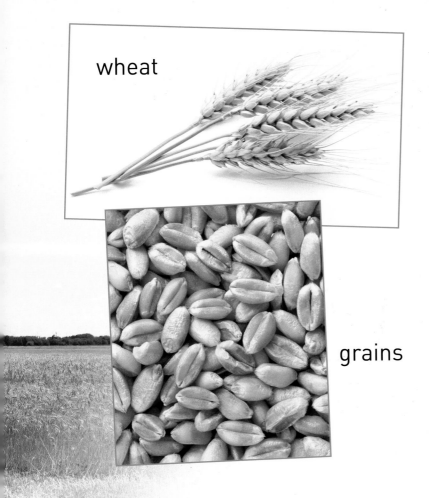

wheat

grains

How do farmers grow wheat?
Let's find out.

Planting the seeds

It's time to plant the seeds. The farmer drives a tractor across the field. The tractor pulls a **plough**. It breaks up big lumps of soil.

Now the farmer can plant the wheat seeds. The tractor pulls a box of seeds across the field. Tiny seeds drop into the soil.

Growing

In the spring, the seeds begin to grow. The new wheat plants push up from the ground. They grow taller and taller.

At the end of the summer, the wheat is golden yellow. It is time to collect the wheat. It's **harvest** time! Here comes the combine harvester!

Harvest time

The combine harvester cuts the wheat. It collects the grains in a tank. It drops the stalks on the ground. We call the stalks **straw**.

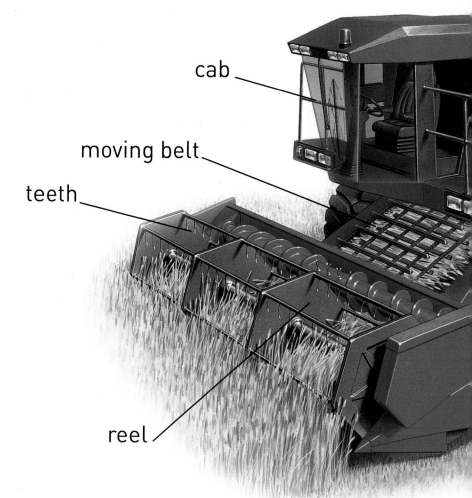

cab

moving belt

teeth

reel

Here are the different parts of a combine harvester.

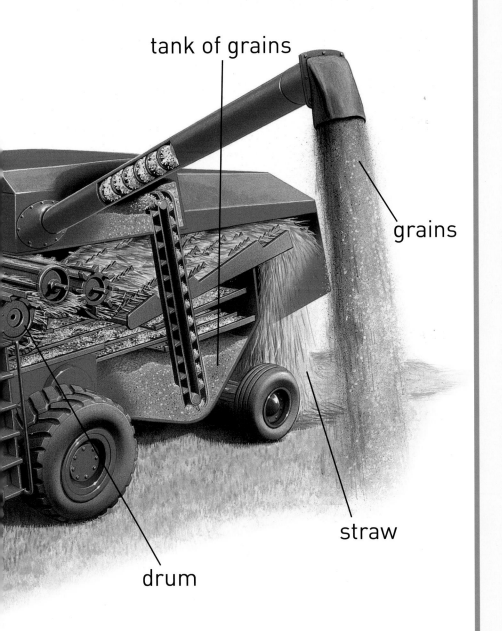

tank of grains

grains

drum

straw

Cutting

The combine harvester has metal teeth on the reel at the front. The teeth pick up wheat from the ground.

The reel moves the wheat towards the **cutter bar** beneath it. The cut stalks of wheat go up a moving belt into the **drum**.

Separating

Inside the combine harvester, the drum separates the grains from the stalks.

The drum spins around and shakes the stalks. The grains fall out of the stalks. They fall into a tank.

grains

The stalks drop
onto the ground
as straw.

straw

drum

tank of grains

To the mill

The tank inside the combine harvester is soon full of grains. The grains pour out of a pipe into a **trailer**. A tractor pulls the trailer to the **mill**.

In the mill, machines crush the grains to make flour. We use flour to make bread, pasta and cakes.

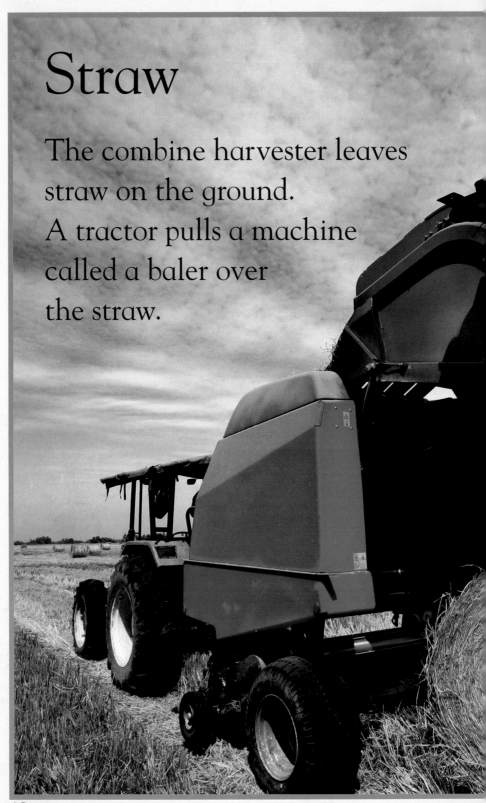

Straw

The combine harvester leaves straw on the ground. A tractor pulls a machine called a baler over the straw.

The baler sucks up the straw and presses it into **bales**. Then it ties the bales with string.

Farm animals will sleep on the straw.

In the cab

The driver of the combine harvester sits inside the **cab**. The cab keeps the driver away from the dust.

People on farms work very hard at harvest time. They drive the combine harvester all day long. Sometimes they drive it at night.

Every day, the driver checks, cleans and fixes the machine.

Field to flour

Now you know how combine harvesters help to turn wheat into flour! Let's look at what happens one more time.

plough the field

plant the seeds

cut the wheat

collect the grains

pour out the grains

crush the grains at the mill

make flour for bread, pasta and cakes

23

In the past

In the past, farmers cut crops and collected the grains by hand. This took a very long time.

Combine harvesters do lots of jobs at once. This saves time.

The first combine harvesters were made about 200 years ago. They were pulled by horses.

Then combine harvesters had engines to make them work.

Around the world

Today, many farmers still cut crops by hand. Farmers in poorer countries do not have enough money to buy combine harvesters.

Combine harvesters can be used for different kinds of crops. Rice is a crop. It grows in wet fields in hot countries. Farmers use a special combine harvester for rice.

Large and small

This is one of the largest combine harvesters in the world. Its cutter bar is almost 11 metres long. That's as long as a bus!

This is the world's smallest combine harvester. You can hold it with two hands!

Combine battle!

It's time for a combine battle! Some farmers paint their old combine harvesters and drive them into each other. They try to burst tyres with their cutter bars.

Smash, crash, bang!

A combine loses the battle if it breaks down or falls apart. The winner is the combine that is still in one piece!

Glossary

bales bundles of straw or hay

cab the place where the driver sits

crops plants grown on a farm for food

cutter bar a long, sharp bar that turns around

drum a big tube that spins around to shake the wheat inside

grains the seeds inside wheat, barley and oat plants

harvest the time when farmers collect crops that are fully grown

mill a building with machines inside that crush grains to make flour

plough a farm tool that cuts into the soil

straw the wheat stalks left behind after collecting the grains

trailer a container on wheels